Lucile M. Marvin

TOWARDS PEACE IN INDO-CHINA

CHATHAM HOUSE ESSAYS

Previous essays in the series have been:

Towards Peace in Indo-China

BY

ANTHONY EDEN
EARL OF AVON

Issued under the auspices of the
Royal Institute of International Affairs
OXFORD UNIVERSITY PRESS
LONDON   KUALA LUMPUR   MELBOURNE
1966

Oxford University Press, Ely House, London W.1.
GLASGOW NEW YORK TORONTO MELBOURNE WELLINGTON
BOMBAY CALCUTTA MADRAS KARACHI LAHORE DACCA
CAPE TOWN SALISBURY NAIROBI IBADAN KUALA LUMPUR HONG KONG

Printed in Great Britain by
The Eastern Press Ltd., Reading

The best hope of one day renewing conversations with the greatest power in the Far East lies in reviving the spirit of the Geneva Agreements. On condition, however, that China renounces making her power, her grudges, her desires and her revolutionary faith the sole laws for Asia today.

JEAN LACOUTURE and PHILIPPE DEVILLERS, *La fin d'une guerre* (Paris, Ed. du Seuil, 1960) (Author's translation).

Contents

Select Documents

Preface

by The Rt. Hon. Kenneth Younger

On behalf of Chatham House, I warmly welcome the opportunity of publishing an essay on the Indo-China problem by Lord Avon, who has for many years been one of the Institute's Presidents.

Lord Avon was one of the principal architects of the Agreements reached at the Geneva Conference on Indo-China in 1954, which marked the end of the period of French colonial rule and opened a new phase in the history of the area. He therefore speaks with especial authority about the considerations which led to the signing of these Agreements and the reasons for the substantial differences of opinion which divided the western powers at that time.

Although twelve years have elapsed since these events, the international machinery established in 1954 is still in existence and the Agreements of that year are still constantly invoked by governments both for purposes of mutual recrimination and as a possible starting point of negotiations for a way out of the present conflict.

In this essay, Lord Avon makes it clear that he is not concerned to allot blame for past mistakes and is recalling past history only in so far as this may help to point the way to future settlement. He asserts that the objectives pursued in 1954 are still the right ones, even if some of the methods then proposed were inadequate and the time-scale in part unrealistic.

Lord Avon's thesis derives enhanced interest from the fact that there is at the present time renewed discussion of the diplomatic techniques by which an area may be rendered neutral in the military confrontation of the great powers, on the basis of temporary acceptance of partition and under mutual great power guarantees. Since the test of such a concept lies largely in the trustworthiness of the guarantees, the renewed consideration of this problem by so experienced a diplomat as Lord Avon has a clear relevance to current thinking.

In undertaking to publish Lord Avon's essay, Chatham House, in accordance with its unvariable custom, presents it as a serious contribution to the study of international affairs, but without adopting the author's opinions, which are his own. The Institute's contribution to the volume has been to add, in agreement with Lord Avon, a selection of texts relevant to the events of 1954 and subsequently, compiled by John Gittings. It is hoped that this may help to set Lord Avon's argument against a background of essential facts which might not otherwise be readily present to his readers' minds.

Foreword

IT is fashionable to date Indo-China's recent history, and most of its troubles, from its colonial past. This is too superficial a reckoning and leaves out of the tally some figures which count for more.

Certain parts of the world have been strategically important for long periods of history. Nuclear warfare may modify this, but since, mercifully, we do not yet have to consider it as dominant in every conflict, the old rules still have their significance.

For centuries the so-called Low Countries were critical strategic areas. In this sense Indo-China has been a cockpit for contending rulers and races. It still is. The earlier rivalry between Indian and Chinese civilizations counts for less in these days, the Indian being so much the weaker. This, however, does not imply that the several countries into which Indo-China is now divided have any natural taste for permanent Chinese rule. The contrary is probably true of the majority of their peoples, even the communists among them, if an alternative to alien rule were available.

By tradition and, I suspect, by inclination if left to themselves, Laos, Cambodia and Vietnam would prefer to be both independent and neutral. Were the concept of such a neutral belt ever realized, it could bring prosperity to these three states and confidence to their neighbours. This was the outcome sought for in the Geneva Agreements of 1954 and, though it did not come about, the purpose was right and as much in the interests of the great powers as in that of the three small states themselves. No great power can now hope to rule all Indo-China with the acceptance of its peoples, even if it has the ambition to do so. Moreover, the United States and China are each convinced that security demands that the other shall not attempt the role. Neutrality is not a crime, it is a risk. Indo-China could be an example where neutrality could also be the way through to peace.

Suggestions by third parties for the settlement of differences are rarely welcome. Yet it is not easy for the central figures of a dispute to stand back and free their judgment from the daily trammels, whether military or political. Thus, though international conferences may not always reach foreseen ends by foreseen means, they can often be fruitful. It was so when representatives of the great powers met, together with the Asian countries involved in the war in Indo-China, at a conference table in 1954. In the end proposals were accepted by the participants, with reservations of varying force by the United States and Diem's newly formed government in South Vietnam. At three o'clock on the twenty-first of July, 1954, the conference was finally adjourned. It had stopped an eight-year war and reduced international tension at a point of instant danger to world peace.

The Geneva Conference fell short, but not by so wide a margin. This essay is an attempt to examine the causes for these shortcomings, set against the background of recent events, and to suggest why the way of 1954 is still that which the world should follow and how we may guard against earlier mistakes. In so doing I have not tried to prove that one nation or another was right or wrong in its past actions. This does not seem to matter, except in so far as it helps us to weigh their consequences fairly and thus end hostilities in conditions which can be something more than a fleeting truce.

AVON

Villa Nova
Barbados
April 1966

Acknowledgement

I wish to express my thanks to Mr Cornelius Dwyer, Jr for his help in the preparation of this book.

CHINA

Kunming

Canton

Hong Kong

Phong Saly

NORTH

BURMA

Dien Bien Phu   Hanoi

Sam Neua   Haiphong

PLAINE DES   GULF OF

JARRES   VIETNAM

HAINAN

TONGKING

MEKONG

LAOS

ANNAM FRANCAISE

Vientiane   Dong Hoi

Boundary

THAILAND   Hué

Da Nang

Bangkok   SOUTH

CAMBODIA   VIETNAM

Phnom Penh

Saigon   CAMRANH

BAY

South China Sea

MALAYA

0   250

MILES

Regmarad

I

How the Second War in Indo-China came about

IN the present situation in South-East Asia the danger of direct conflict between the United States and China is real. There is, I think, a tendency in the Anglo-Saxon world to underestimate this danger, which will not grow less just because the war in Vietnam makes us familiar with it. The reverse is nearer the truth.

The Chinese have many qualities, among which industry holds a leading place. In negotiation, however, they are never in a hurry and it takes time to fathom their intention. It is not so much that the Chinese conceal it, as that their minds and methods set their thoughts in a different perspective. Nor is it easy to weigh the depth or the sincerity of their convictions. In spite of which one Chinese article of faith is all too genuinely held, the belief that the United States is implacably hostile. To this alleged ambition to destroy the Chinese communist state, is attributed every American move of recent years, whether off the China coast or elsewhere in South-East Asia.

It is not necessary to recapitulate events to show how this deeply held suspicion has sought and found confirmation. Inspired perhaps by American support of Chiang Kai-Shek's resistance to the communist takeover in 1949, it was reinforced by the debate which took place during the 1952 Presidential campaign in the United States.

From this it appeared that the Republican leaders and their supporters were at least considering whether they should sanction an invasion of the Chinese mainland by Chiang Kai-Shek. Wiser heads might regard such proposals as extravagant; they would be notched up none the less in Chinese memories as intentions which they believed all Americans to harbour.

Whatever the cause, the chief Chinese opposition during the 1954 negotiations at Geneva was to any American military presence, however innocuous in itself, within any territories of the three states of Indo-China. The activities of the United States, the Chinese argued, were directed against them and not in defence of the territories which the United States was professing to help.

The Chinese response to our attempts at the Conference to agree upon a military mission to train the Royal Laotian army was an example of this stubborn denial of any American good intention. After many weeks of argument Mr Chou En-Lai told me one morning in June that he thought he could persuade the Vietminh to withdraw from Laos and Cambodia. China would then recognize the Royal Governments, on condition that there were no American bases in the territories. The problem of training the Laotian army remained and, after another spell of several weeks of argument, was finally resolved. It was agreed that the French Government should keep their two military bases in Laos and that these should be exempted from the general withdrawal of foreign troops from the country. There was at no time any hope that even one American military base might be allowed instead.

This outcome may not seem so surprising now, at a time when large American forces are in Vietnam. In 1954, however, France was still the colonial power against whose forces the communists had, until a few weeks before, been fighting a particularly bloody war on a large scale and over a period of years. In this business the Americans had taken no direct military part except through the French, whom they supplied with weapons and sustained with credits. Yet the military presence of the colonial power was to be preferred to that of the Americans, which had to be resisted even to the point of jeopardizing the agreements. I had no doubt then, and have none now, that this attitude was once again evidence of the incurable Chinese conviction that the United States intended a day of reckoning for them in its own time.

Anything which I could and did say, then or later, to the Chinese representatives to deny this false assumption failed to sway their judgment. Theirs was not a suspicion, it was a faith which was unhappily confirmed by occasional incursions from Washington, or on Washington's instructions, when the Geneva Conference was in a critical phase. These were difficult to interpret except as impatience or as reluctance to see the Conference succeed.

General Bedell Smith did everything a man could do and more to align himself with the French and British representatives at Geneva. Even he had to heed his Government's instructions for the final session. These were that the United States was not prepared to join the Conference declaration, but would take note of the agreements, would refrain from the threat or the use of force to disturb them and would view any renewal of the aggression in violation of them as seriously threatening international peace and security.[1] This ambiguous American attitude

[1] See below, p. 46.

caused many perplexities for the non-communist delegations who wanted to stay as close to the United States as
possible, but could not renege on their work. One strata-
gem we had to devise was to list the Governments represented at the Conference at the opening of the final
document in order to camouflage the American refusal to
sign.[2] These and other manoeuvres which were more
involved than successful did not, of course, pass unob-
served. They served further to convince the Chinese that
their view of American intentions was the right one.

The events of the summer of 1954 inevitably aroused
controversy in the United States, as elsewhere. One of the
most mordant of the Administration's critics was Senator
Lyndon B. Johnson who was, a decade later and in a
position of greater authority, to be called upon to face a
situation influenced by the decisions of that earlier period.
He said, 'American foreign policy has never in all its
history suffered such a stunning reversal. . . . We stand in
clear danger of being left naked and alone in a hostile
world.'[3]

Soon after the Geneva Conference, the President of the
United States wrote to Ngo Dinh Diem, who had recently
become Prime Minister of the southern half of truncated
Vietnam, promising his country's support 'to assist the
Government of Vietnam in developing and maintaining a
strong, viable state'.[4] This state was to be capable of
resisting attempted subversion or aggression through
military means. From that time the American commitment to South Vietnam and to Diem became firm, deeply

[2] See below p. 49.
[3] *New York Times*, 7 May 1954.
[4] See below, p. 52.

felt and increasingly independent. Mr. Arthur Schlesinger's judgment that the mood in which Washington began the Vietnam adventure was essentially 'moralistic' is, I believe, true.[5] Equally justified is his comment that the anti-colonial mood of the Secretary of State required the commitment to be in the main an American one, 'lest', writes Mr. Schlesinger, 'our effort in South Vietnam be tainted by suspicions of European imperialism'.[6]

Later that year the decision was taken by the United States to reduce drastically the payments made to France for Indo-China and to begin direct financial aid to the Independent States on January 1st, 1955. Though this was plausible enough, so sharp a switch had the inevitable consequence of forcing an early reduction in the strength of French forces in Indo-China. Henceforth it was only a question of how long a final withdrawal must take.

This was a misfortune, because French influence, under the wise and friendly guidance of General Ely, who had been named High Commissioner and Commander-in-Chief, could have been helpful both to Diem and to the United States. Ely was a convinced and devoted supporter of the Western Alliance, who had served on many missions to Washington and was well known there. His experience and sympathy would have been invaluable in guiding those who were new to the country and in restraining Diem's more extreme policies. He foresaw only too clearly the consequences to which unconditional support of Diem must lead, but while the American Ambassador might heed his advice locally, Washington had charted its course and was in no mood to listen. So Ely came away.

---

[5] *A Thousand Days* (London, Deutsch, 1965), p. 536.
[6] Ibid., p. 537.

We can be sure that the Chinese watched this change of overlords and made their own reckoning, which included to their minds evidence that the United States wished to play its own hand in South Vietnam untrammelled by any Western associate.

Even so, Diem's efforts, supported by American aid, then mainly economic, did have their period of relative success. The communists recognized it as such and made their plans accordingly; those who once supported Diem so unquestioningly should give him that recognition now.

In his first two years, until the late autumn of 1956, Diem's rule was bold and effective within certain limits. Fervent patriot and ardent Catholic though he was, austere in his habits and incorruptible, these qualities were not enough, even if they had been repeated in his family which shared power with him. Had Diem been able to broaden his appeal, he might have proved too strong for the Vietcong; but this was not in him, nor imposed upon him.

Two deadly failings should early have been apparent. The army was not trained from the start for the kind of warfare it was most likely to meet, guerrilla fighting. Some valuable years were wasted, with the result that when the Vietcong resumed operations in 1959, the government forces had to devise new methods. The lessons learnt by the French the hard way had to be learnt the same way all over again. Added to this was a consequence of Diem's arbitrary rule. Officers regarded as politically trustworthy by his brother, Ngo Dinh Nhu, and himself were selected for important military commands and they were not always the best men for the job. The United States had chosen some brave and devoted officers to train and go into action with South Vietnamese units. These failures in command were for them often frustrating and sometimes fatal.

Equally grave in its consequences was Diem's inability to understand or promote the welfare of the peasant farmer. There were paper plans and assurances in plenty but no effective action. The scope of Diem's appeal narrowed, his relations with the Buddhists became clouded, and so it continued with deterioration until his fall.

By a coincidence 1956, which was perhaps Diem's best year, was the worst for the communists and those under their rule in North Vietnam. Plagued by food shortages and peasant uprisings against collectivism, it was politically and economically unhappy. Neither prolonged fighting nor American bombing has yet brought the North back to that nadir. This state of affairs may have influenced the relatively modest pressure from communist sources for the elections of 1956, which had been foreshadowed in the Geneva Agreements.[7] There were protests, of course, at any suggestion of delay, but these were hardly vehement, nor championed with any fervent conviction by the sponsoring communist powers, notably Soviet Russia, whose Government are ever chary of even the slightest electoral risk.

Certain dates must now be set down, because, whatever the counter-claim, they have helped to create the present conflict and suffering. '[From] 1954 to '59, the two parts of Viet-Nam lived, uneasily indeed, but at least in comparative peace', said the British Foreign Secretary, Mr

[7] See below, p. 53.

Stewart, at Oxford in June 1965.[8] This is true, even though the Vietcong was in existence on a limited scale in 1958 and some of its elements had never withdrawn to the North after the Geneva Agreements, preferring, or being instructed, to go underground. It was not until September, 1960 that the Communist party of North Vietnam declared itself by calling for the 'liberation of South Vietnam from American imperialism' and not until December that the Vietcong set up a National Liberation Front.

Admittedly, North Vietnam had been supplying equipment and encouraging, and maybe ordering, men to cross the demarcation line and join up with the Vietcong before that date, but the scale had been comparatively small. Curiously enough, this action was made the easier by the Geneva Agreements which provided for an exchange of population, a merciful arrangement which resulted in a considerable flow of families either way. As a consequence, there was by 1959 a sufficient proportion of South Vietnamese living in the North, but sharing the political sentiments of the Vietcong, which could sincerely combine both a communist and a nationalist faith.

Diem's deeds of repression played into communist hands, even though they were exceeded in 1960 by the Vietcong's torture and execution of village leaders, wherever they could contrive it over wide and disparate areas of the country.

These methods, and a well-armed and directed policy of infiltration, soon obscured the immediate influence of American aid and destroyed any present hope of comparison between rising standards of life in the South and

[8] *Documents relating to British Involvement in the Indo-China Conflict, 1945-65,* Cmnd. 2834 (1966), p. 263.

rigid ones in the North. Without doubt a determination that this contrast should not appear was a motive for what Mr Stewart has called the 'deliberate decision by the Communist North to make an attack on its neighbour'.[9] It should be added that the American imperialism against which communist propaganda became so fervent from 1960 onwards, consisted at the time of financial aid and weapons and military instruction. Combatant troops were not introduced until 1965, though their numbers then soon multiplied speedily. The first incursion by North Vietnamese combat forces must be dated several years earlier.

The pattern has changed little to this day; the South buttressed by American help, but still lacking a positive political message or example, the North fanatic in faith but scarcely allowing life or breath to any other creed or party.

The problem now is whether the terms of any association can be devised which will give security to the area and confidence to the two great powers whose deeper involvement and sharper conflict could be a calamity for mankind. It is my belief that they can.

[9] Ibid.

2

Peking and Hanoi

IN its intransigence Hanoi has received thus far the undeviating support of Peking. There are many western theories as to the true purpose of Chinese policy in Indo-China. One which is specious and popular argues that Peking is well content with things as they are in North and South Vietnam. The United States is now heavily involved there by land and air, yet can see no end to its costly military commitment which, so the contention runs, does the American name and fame no good.

Admittedly, Chinese intentions may have been modified since 1954, but not, in my opinion, as drastically as this. If the active hostility of the American purpose is a fixed belief in the Chinese mind, no tar-baby theory could compensate for so powerful a concentration of American force so near at hand. It is not that fear determines Chinese policy, on the contrary, probably no nation is more unafraid, but a natural geographical reaction which we should all share if we happened to harbour Peking's delusion about the United States. It is as if the China lobby of ten or fifteen years ago represented the American people today; the two scarcely speak the same language.

There is still less excuse for the Chinese to regard President Johnson as an eager belligerent. The President has inherited a sack of troubles which he had much rather be without, but he cannot just ditch it. He knows that if he jettisons his responsibilities, the consequences are quite literally incalculable. This has not kept him from repeating, since his Baltimore speech of April, 1965, that the United States Government are prepared to negotiate without conditions.

The American interest would probably accept a neutral belt as fulfilling its needs, but the assurances that it would be observed would have to be as complete as human ingenuity can make them. It may be that from their own angle the Chinese are not so far from the same position. Even when either side can reasonably accept a solution with which the other can be content, a wide gulf of mistrust may still divide the principals. It was, I think, one of the famous Cambon family of ambassadors who declared that mistrust has done more mischief in diplomacy than over-confidence. That is an arguable proposition, but if the international situation is approximately as we have described, it remains highly perilous, but not necessarily insoluble.

So far the President has played patiently and resisted pressure, which is statesmanship, for while, I believe, China will not seek an enlargement of the war, neither will she flee from it, so that the field of manoeuvre may not be large.

Meanwhile the danger is rather that each country, the United States and China, should become fixed and determined in an erroneous conviction of the other's policy. That could bring us to disaster. As an Englishman I know that the Chinese are wrong in supposing that the present Administration in the United States wants to keep American troops in South-East Asia. Even the immense expenditures at Camranh Bay and elsewhere do not spell

permanency in American eyes. They could find their place
in the expanding economy of the areas which they are now
designed to serve militarily.

I do not feel able to dogmatize about Chinese policy;
Mr Nehru's confidence which was to be so sadly shaken at
the end, and the phobia of the American China lobby,
were neither of them convincing to me. The obligation
remains to try to promote a settlement which, if it suc-
ceeds, can prove to each party that its extreme convictions
of the evil intentions of the other are not justified. There is
a fair chance that this may be the truth. On balance we
can still assume that Peking would be glad to see the last
American soldier and airman leave Indo-China, but on
what terms remains to be discussed.

China's conduct on its other frontiers has been chequered and hardly reassuring. Tibet has suffered an act of
conquest. Neither its people nor those of India, with their
own taste of Chinese aggressiveness, can be expected to
interpret or excuse these acts as part of an old imperialism
or as a border foray.

The truth is that while there is much that is disturbing
about Chinese foreign policy there is also much that is
equivocal. A critical question mark hovers over it. We
cannot unhappily exclude the hypothesis that China's
policy may be grimly expansionist. Our duty is to prepare
plans providing international guarantees for the security
of a neutral belt and offer the Chinese Government their
full part in them. Experience in the working of these
guarantees has to be earned; there is no escape from that
if we want to limit and halt this war.

It may be, of course, that the Chinese Government see

the contest in Vietnam chiefly as a phase of the 'revolutionary war', American aggressive intentions being discounted. If this were so, Peking should have more elasticity in its negotiating position.

If, for instance, the Chinese Government's chief interest in Indo-China is to ensure the security of North Vietnam, a scheme of neutralization for its southern neighbors might have its attractions. Peking would not regard any such arrangement as other than temporary, for it would no doubt count upon the success of propaganda among Buddhist, intellectual, and even nationalist elements in South Vietnam as certain to ensure a Vietcong victory in time. Meanwhile, however, a neutralized area in South Vietnam, Laos and Cambodia might be acceptable in the interest of the North. Even if Peking's calculations of ultimate victory in South Vietnam were delayed or proved false, as well they might be, this would not appear so disastrous an event if compensated by a neutral South and the reduction and finally the departure of American troops.

If, on the other hand, communist China's obsession with early victory in this 'war of national liberation' proves so strong as to surpass any fear of American forces on its Southern flank, or any concern for the limited capacity of the Vietcong, or even of North Vietnam, in the face of growing United States military strength, another consideration has to be weighed. In such conditions, would Hanoi be prepared indefinitely to 'fight to the last drop of Vietnamese blood' to prove a communist theory so dear to the Chinese?

For Ho Chi Minh the pursuit of the union of the two Vietnams, which he has faith must be the ultimate outcome of the conflict however long it is postponed, could be of more account than the problematic future of the international communist revolution. For Hanoi and Peking, as for Washington, the solution of a neutralized area in Indo-China could have a growing appeal, not as realizing all the hopes of any one of them, but as a compromise which would fairly safeguard their principal security needs in the area. For all interested parties this solution might only be accepted as a staging post, the world would not be the loser if it became a permanent place of rest.

If Peking is obsessed by its wrongful impression of American intentions, Hanoi's opinion may eventually prove less decided. Moscow's judgment has influence in North Vietnam which can at times balance Peking's. If China's support is the tougher and more resolutely proclaimed, a number of Hanoi's communist leaders are Moscow trained, including Ho Chi Minh himself. Moreover, historic instincts can be strong, however Left the leaders. The Vietnamese might not relish a fate which could relegate them to serve as China's southernmost imperial outpost, even for a time.

There are risks also for North Vietnam in the growing Sino-Soviet bitterness. Recently the Chinese Government have even ignored all anniversaries of friendship with their Soviet ally, however revered previously. Peking makes the Vietnam campaign a cause of complaint against Russia, while dawdling Soviet supplies on their journey. That is not cosy for Hanoi which has no wish to quarrel with either communist great power, but could find the extreme Chinese demands increasingly prickly to live with.

The parallel which is sometimes drawn between Marshal Tito and Moscow and Ho Chi Minh and Peking is not, however, close. North Vietnam is at war and in no position to quarrel with its chief provider of arms and supplies. Even in less arduous conditions, China would still be the big neighbour, as well as the big brother, and difficult to defy, if such a thing could be even dreamt of. All the same there is more scope for eventual agreement with Hanoi than with Peking, despite the tragic trail of blood and suffering, or maybe because of it.

It is Vietnam, not China, which has had the losses in life and in wealth, from schools to communications. Some day, somehow, this has to end. Moreover, even the North has much to gain from forming part of a girdle of neutral states, or at least from seeing such a girdle formed to the south and south-west of its territory. For this to be possible Hanoi must accept two glimpses of reality, though they need never be publicly proclaimed. The first is that the United States cannot be beaten, the second is that while a United States military withdrawal might find its place in a phased time-table within an agreement, there is not a remote chance of even a partial American withdrawal unless North Vietnam plays its part, although a negative one, to make this possible.

Admittedly, the National Liberation Front may have both a loyal following and a momentum of its own. This could make difficulties, whatever the attitude of Peking and Hanoi, but only for a while. Local resources and captured supplies would not be enough to keep the fight going indefinitely. Hanoi's leverage gives it the power to decide.

It could be different if the Vietcong were winning more

results, or enjoyed more panache in the communist world. Though brave guerrilla fighters, they are holding their own militarily and nothing more; politically their message is growing musty. Peking scarcely conceals its dissatisfaction on this score, yet, rather surprisingly, seems unable or unwilling to do much about it.

The inelasticity of the Vietcong has been as limiting a factor as the lack of political inspiration among the Government's leaders. The combination of the two, while it reduces the chances of outright victory for either side, does not necessarily add up to another obstacle to a settlement. The closer the warring factions can get to an understanding of what cannot be won, the sooner will modest reason have a chance again.

It may be that in spite of, or even because of, the economic dislocation it has caused, the bombing of North Vietnam has created in the inhabitants an illusion of being David against Goliath. This has often been so, in Britain in 1940, in Germany when the allied attacks grew heavier, more recently in the Yemen, where there was scarcely an anti-aircraft gun to crack against the Egyptian bombers. It is certain that the air attacks are regarded by the North Vietnamese with hatred, not merely on account of the casualties but also because, where in the Far East the margin of subsistence is already narrow, destruction which narrows it further is considered the harshest cruelty.

Even so, the North Vietnamese Government would be wise to take a tally of the odds. If it cannot win militarily, it could also lose out politically in South Vietnam if the American hand there is played intelligently.

An Englishman might also tender some advice from his reading of American history. The Civil War was characteristic in the early set-backs, as at Bull-run, and the time taken by the North to limber up. So now effort may be misdirected at first, but once in its stride, the momentum will be hard to check.

From one point of view Russia might be considered as the country with most to gain by continued fighting in Vietnam. Whatever the immediate exigencies of Soviet foreign policy, the United States is still the leading capitalist power and the citadel of free enterprise. It could therefore be tempting to see that country as deeply enmeshed as possible in Indo-China, because it is unfortunately true that, despite vast American resources, preoccupation with Vietnam could weaken Washington's watchfulness in other continents where the stakes are higher.

For the Soviets, however, still more formidable considerations of national interest must prevail. Moscow will do everything in its power to prevent the fighting in Indo-China from spreading into a third world war. Should that peril draw nearer, Soviet diplomacy will become correspondingly more active, which could entail a revival of serious co-operation between the two co-chairmen of the Geneva Conference, Russia and Britain. It was so in 1954 and the experience could be repeated. Meanwhile there are dangers in the despatch of modern MIG fighters to North Vietnam. Moscow may think this necessary to assert 'local' influence and eclipse Peking, but the attendant risks will multiply.

The Soviet Government have shown a consistent

interest in the position accorded them as a co-chairman at the Geneva Conference, which is one of the reasons for continuing the arrangements laid down there and offering Soviet diplomacy its chance.

Another motive for using the Conference machinery is that China has never yet won sufficient votes to secure admission to the United Nations. While Peking would presumably welcome membership, no Chinese government, communist or otherwise, would be willing to pay a price for what they regard as a right. In such conditions it would probably be prudent not to attempt to inject the United Nations into negotiations at the present stage.

Let us hope that Moscow is also mindful that the diffusion of the conflict could come suddenly, allowing diplomacy little scope, and that it is a dreadful responsibility to leave the world at the edge of risk if anything can be done to draw it back. Here, however, Russian diplomacy is vexed and impeded by the Sino-Soviet quarrel. Moscow will be infinitely reluctant to take any step which could be pilloried as showing less enthusiasm than Peking for Hanoi's cause at any given moment. Admittedly the role is a difficult one, but it will not get easier and may have to be played lest the worst befall.

What is needed now is some dilution of the conflict, so that we can travel for a while in the opposite direction to the ever more intense fighting of recent years. That will not come about from war weariness alone, though after more than twenty years of hostilities this influence might surely play its part. Two other components are indispensable. The first, a project for a peace settlement which is clear and yet in sufficiently detailed pattern to carry conviction. The second, a succession of military moves which could be related to this pattern, so that the spring can be unwound, not just as a temporary accident but as part of a prepared scheme of things.

3

Guarantees

No agreement can be so drawn as to be proof against every malevolent intention. That is why the observance of international engagements is the first condition of any peaceful society. Once allow treaties to be torn up with impunity and the world is headed for trouble; violators soon have imitators.

All of which underlines the importance of building as well-founded an agreement as we can in Indo-China and buttressing it soundly. Three conditions appear indispensable. First, that any arrangement takes account of the will of at least two of the territories and guarantees the neutrality of Laos and Cambodia, offering the same opportunities to South and North Vietnam. This guarantee should be endorsed by the principal powers represented at Geneva in 1954, and preferably by all of them.

Secondly, the Geneva precedents should be followed whenever possible, if only because the communist powers have shown a firm will to have it this way and there is no sufficient reason why they should not be met. On the contrary, some ingredients could be strengthened to give better results. For instance, there is probably advantage in the limited membership of the Geneva Conference.[1] Though the direct interest in the area of some of the powers

[1] Cambodia, France, Laos, North and South Vietnam, the People's Republic of China, the U.S.S.R, United Kingdom and United States.

has grown since 1954, while that of others has waned, the mixture as a whole is much as before, which is all to the good. Moreover, certain of the machinery which the Conference set up, by intent or hazard, can be made to serve to better purpose.

Thirdly, the greatest importance must attach to the supervision of any agreement reached. This was a stumbling block in 1954 and could prove to be so again. My own strong preference would be to keep the membership of the Commission as it is today. The three countries, India, Canada and Poland are admirably balanced politically and have as much chance of reaching a common judgment as any other three powers which could be named to do the job. They have had some years' experience of working together and, despite their limited powers, have enjoyed, here and there, some success. They are familiar with the territories and the work to be done.

On this occasion, however, their powers must be clearly defined and strengthened. The Commission must also have in its terms of reference an obligation to report to the Conference powers, though, in the first instance, this contact had better be made through an accepted and existing channel.

When it was first proposed that the Geneva Conference should appoint two co-chairmen, there was no idea of perpetuating this arrangement beyond the life of that Conference. The Geneva meeting had been called to deal with two wars, Indo-China and Korea. Evidently it would only cause confusion to have rotating chairmen to preside over each conference, the membership of which was not the same. Nor would the representative of any one power have been accepted to preside over either conference.

Hence the proposal that Mr Molotov and I should be co-chairmen of both. This working in double harness having proved tolerable to all concerned, it seemed natural to me to propose at the last meeting of the Indo-China Conference that the troublesome, but minor, business of who was to deal with the financial costs of the arrangements we had made, should be left to the co-chairmen. [2]

As a result of this accident the co-chairmen continued their joint existence, though there was no statutory authority for them. On balance we should, I think, gain by retaining this arrangement, if the other countries interested are prepared to endorse it. This time, the duties of the chairmen towards the Conference and their relationship to the Commission should be clearly laid down. Both they and the Commission will also need a secretariat.

None of these arrangements need imply that the United Nations will be excluded from work in the area. On the contrary, the most hopeful development there is taking place under its auspices and needs to be pushed forward with all possible speed. The scheme to use the waters of the Mekong river to bring prosperity to those who live in the region can be the key to the future of Laos, Cambodia and Vietnam. If once the bold schemes now being blueprinted can be executed, bringing with them a rising standard of living where there has been so much poverty, the minds of men and women may become less attentive to the cries of rival ideologies. This should be a tolerable evolution in countries where, for some of the population at least, neutrality is a natural bent.

Geography dictates that in the first instance the benefits

[2] See below, p. 48.

of the Mekong scheme, in support of which President Johnson and the United States Government have shown generosity and imagination, will accrue to Laos, Thailand, Cambodia and South Vietnam. In time, however, they would percolate further afield to North Vietnam. The political significance of this project is that it will set going centripetal forces in the territories which need them most. Economically those areas could then become an attraction because of their unity, instead of a political temptation to conflict because of their division. If so, their neighbours are not likely to be long impervious to such an appeal.

All counsels therefore seem to join in the chorus: press on with the Mekong plans and any others that can raise the standard of life in the area.

The trade of both North and South Vietnam suffered severely when the territory was divided. That was inevitable, the two halves being economically complementary, with the minerals mainly in the north and the food production in the south. The fighting and bombing of recent years have made matters infinitely worse, but a recovering southern economy, joined with neighbours in a Mekong scheme rich in promise, could prove a magnet for the North. It might even result in less intransigence one day, but not just yet. It would be a mistake to try to go too fast.

We have to remember this when we come to consider plans for the eventual unity of North and South Vietnam. These cannot be rushed without the risk, amounting almost to a certainty, of disaster. Too much has happened; there has been a surfeit of agony and upheaval. Time and the soothing balm of economic recovery must be given a chance. A short span of two or three years before elections to determine Vietnam's future would give none of these influences their scope. All would be intent on the imminent political contest, neither governments nor people would have a mind to relax or rebuild. Charges and counter-charges, incidents real or magnified, manoeuvring for an early decision would keep leaders and followers taut and on a picket line. This would afford the territories nothing better than a harassed truce, with little gained from years of war and suffering. Political man must be offered some solace, but not at the cost of all hope.

There can be little doubt now that the brief two years allowed by the Geneva Agreements before an election in all Vietnam was altogether too short. Some of us thought so at the time, but the pressure from the North was strong and even the French, with their intimate knowledge of the country, had once been willing to accept eighteen months. We must not make that mistake again or we shall per-petuate conflict while there is still too strong a swell upon the waters. There is no possibility of a short-term neutral-ization scheme; the same is not necessarily true of a long.

Ten years, or preferably fifteen, should be allowed to pass before South and North Vietnam are asked to decide upon unity or otherwise with each other. As a compensa-tion to the optimists or the impatient, I would add this proviso, that the term can at any time be shortened with the unanimous agreement of the parties, the co-chairmen and the Commission.

However skilfully all this is worked out, it is doubtful if it will be enough. We need to search for a further under-taking, wrapped up in every contrivance of guarantee, to give confidence to those who want it and warning to those who need it. It is arguable how far deep suspicion of each other's intentions has prodded intervention in Vietnam. Whether on this account or to halt ambitious plans of conquest, every means must be used to allay mistrust and to scotch aggression. It is essential that the parties to the agreement guarantee it, but the form of the guarantee is also important. It should be joint and several and, in order to create the most effective deterrent value, the guarantors must have the right in certain conditions to act without waiting for unanimity, should the terms of the agreement be violated.

The result would be a system of the Locarno type, and, in order to bring it into being in South-East Asia, a number of difficulties would have to be resolved, but the effort would be worthwhile. For the United States such an arrangement would involve joining in a guarantee to which communist China was itself a party. It would also mean for both countries the choice of some organization before whom any alleged breach could be argued. The Security Council of the United Nations is an evident possibility in this connection, but it could be that some body of more local character, though including the great powers, perhaps with a membership comparable to that of the Geneva Conference of 1954, or the later conference on Laos in 1962, would be found more suitable.

As an additional safeguard, the guaranteed countries could be denied the purchase of arms from any of the guarantor powers. This prohibition could be supervised by the Commission.

What is indispensable is that we should use our ingenuity to persuade the world and these small countries of our joint determination to give them a neutral character and to safeguard this condition.

The difficulties speak for themselves only too easily but, if once a system of this kind were established, it might gain authority and momentum, until all found it more advantageous to cling to its benefits than to try to overset it, with all the attendant dangers.

4

Stratagems

IN the conditions of fighting which prevail in Vietnam it would scarcely be practicable to attempt a cease-fire without preliminaries. A conference would first have to give instructions to the military commanders to enable them to disentangle their forces and concentrate them in the appointed areas.

The most intricate of all questions in fighting of this guerrilla character has now to be considered, whether there is any military action which it is possible and prudent for the American authorities to take which would at the same time effectively reduce tension in the area. This problem is further complicated by the limits imposed through the restriction of South Vietnamese and American authority mainly to the towns, whereas the Vietcong controls most of the countryside by day or by night. Obviously the United States and the South Vietnamese should not be asked to take risks which would imperil all they have fought for. Some moves may, however, be feasible, even though they have to be made cautiously and their development is dependent upon acquiescence, if not reciprocity, on the other side.

Bombing is an evident example. The bombing of North Vietnam, with the limitations which the United States has rightly felt compelled to impose,[1] has always been of

[1] I refer to the limitations in force in March 1966.

debatable value. Its influence on the actual fighting is probably more remote than its protagonists will admit. This reservation also applies to attempts to disrupt Vietcong supply lines in South Vietnam and in Laos by air action, or even to bombing attacks by day on road blocks set up by the Vietcong. However complete the devastation, the effect is temporary and therefore not decisive. The belief that one air strike could succeed in fouling the enemy's communications before Dien Bien Phu never seemed to me credible in 1954. I suspect that in the conditions of the present fighting in Vietnam, the claims for the military, as apart from the horror, influence of bombing are also exaggerated.

However that may be, the bombing strategy could be moderated by stages to make such a reduced programme tell in the minds of the enemy. Its effect would be the more compelling, if the successive steps were linked to parallel or related moves by the ground forces.

Here much must depend upon the course of hostilities and the political progress which the United States and the South Vietnamese authorities, whether local or national, can realize in the next few months. We know that the United States has no wish to appear as a colonial power in Vietnam nor to assume a parental role, even for a spell. In spite of this reluctance, some responsibility to guide and guard cannot be avoided and was, indeed, accepted by Vice-President Humphrey's mission to South Vietnam after President Johnson's Hawaii conference in February, 1966.

Whatever new efforts are made, they need not imply that the United States must devote itself to setting up a democratic state in South Vietnam. We should like it much better that way, but we know the obstacles. It remains true that a freely elected Parliamentary democracy is the only effective safeguard to protect the liberty of the individual. While firmly convinced of this, we have unhappily to accept that many in these days still pay lip service to such a form of government, but few have the will or experience to practise it. It is altogether too testing a business.

It would, therefore, be unjust and unreasonable to complain that the United States has not been able to nurture a democratic system, as we understand it, in South Vietnam. An unjaundiced view of Africa and Asia is sufficient reply to such a demand. It is, however, indispensable that an administration which has sufficient support nationally and locally to command a positive following should come into being in South Vietnam. There is no doubt of the deep hatred for communist rule sincerely felt by many South Vietnamese, often as a result of personal experience. Yet it will never be easy to enlist this hostility, which can be due to a variety of causes, except by leadership which has a national appeal.

This is the inescapable political problem for the Americans and their allies, and no doubt the Americans know it. As for the South Vietnamese, their endurance has been heroic and they deserve a solution which will at last bring peace to their mauled countryside.

While a more widely based political authority is constantly being sought in the South, this result would be encouraged if all military action in the country were, as far as possible, co-ordinated to serve the main political purpose, the promotion of unity. This will entail the

patient protection of an increasing number of selected
country areas and the encouragement of local administration and leadership within them. It will be no easy
task where the Vietcong can move so effectively by night,
but it has to be done, for no solution is possible based on
the effective guardianship of towns alone. However long
it takes, methodically settled conditions must be brought,
stage by stage, to selected parts of the countryside. They
must be given the chance to live and breathe; nothing
can be accomplished without this. For the people it is not
a question of being for or against the Vietcong; it is
survival. It was so in Malaya and, no doubt, the same rules
apply in the more difficult conditions of Vietnam.

When regions of assured security have been established
by day and night, a further step in evolution will be in
sight. Certain definable areas of the country should then
enjoy conditions which are sufficiently stable for a local
withdrawal of American forces to be practicable without
undue risk; South Vietnamese forces could remain. If we
travel this far successfully, we might be at the turning
point.

Such a withdrawal could be announced as well as made.
Supposing these events produced no unfavourable
reaction, the way would be open to repeat the tactics in
another part of the country. It might then be that the
confidence gained by the South Vietnamese and their
solid survival over a period of time, would make it safe
for the United States Government to order a first withdrawal of one of their units from Vietnam. This would be
retreat by trial and success.

Admittedly, the outcome could be very different. The
Vietcong might, if it were militarily in their scope to do so,

seize the occasion to launch an attack on the chosen area. If this succeeded, the American trial experiment would have been an apparent failure. If, however, the attempt were foiled, the Vietcong would suffer grievously in reputation as well as in fact. In either event such tactics would be hard to reconcile with Vietcong claims that all that was wanted was the withdrawal of the Americans, when hostilities would cease and every problem be resolved. On balance, therefore, this method, or an adaptation of it, seems worth following. It is important to take political ground from the Vietcong; the conditions for a settlement will not be lined up by military means alone.

The odds are evidently against the success of such a scheme as this, but not overwhelmingly so. I have seen other situations which at some time have looked equally bleak but which later yielded to a solution. This is the reason why it is important to show by practice that every obligation to which the free world is pledged is kept, whatever the behaviour of the Vietcong. Prominent among these is the Geneva Prisoners of War Convention.

Mankind has made progress in science in this century, in mercy it has moved backwards. Torture was little practised and much frowned upon among nations which still called themselves civilized a hundred years ago. This adjective may seem arrogant to modern ears, but I do not think that it was. Torture is debasing and sadistic and it is a sorrowful mark of the times in which we live that it should be tolerated in war and so constantly publicized in peace. It was to establish a code of conduct for the humane treatment of prisoners of war that the

Geneva Convention was accepted; it has to be respected if a claim to uphold the rule of law is to have any meaning.

There is also a military side to this question. Those of us who have served with combat troops know that if anything is likely to stiffen a man's determination to soldier on to the end, it is the knowledge that he will be tortured if he is captured. The western purpose in Vietnam is to get the enemy to the conference table. Everything that can be done to convince the civilian population that they will be well cared for if they transfer allegiance, and the fighting man that the rules of war will protect him if he surrenders, will bring us nearer that day.

It is, however, only the known practice, not the promise of these benefits, that will weigh in the scales. Generous treatment of prisoners can tell quite heavily, as it did in Malaya and the Philippines, and should be the rule, whatever the Oriental opinion of torture. What we want to establish are conditions in which bitterness can be mollified and hatred assuaged.

Admittedly, these suggestions cannot determine the conflict in so far as it is one between the free world and the communist world. The most they can do is to help provide a compromise, an accommodation with which both sides can learn to live. There have been many such in history. Then perhaps these territories can cease to be 'a point of instant danger to world peace',[2] as I had hoped when the Geneva Conference closed in the summer of 1954. Whether we can do better this time depends not merely on the ingenuity of our plans, but also on whether the principals have a mind to give them a chance to work.

[2] See below, p. 49.

5

Two Natural Neutrals

The Laotians

THERE is surely a moral in the recent history of Laos.
A sparse population inhabits a lonely, mountainous
country and asks only that the world should pass it by.
It is possible to mock the Laotians because they differ so
much from the warlike hill tribes of tradition, the Scottish
Highlanders of the eighteenth century or the Pathans of a
later date; it is also possible to respect them.

I first felt sympathy for these people at the 1954 Geneva
Conference, because they differed from all others in their
approach to their problems. They appeared to harbour
neither resentment nor suspicion against their neighbours,
nor even to take much interest in them. Stranger still,
they seemed quite free of any ideological fervour, neither
to want to be communists, nor to wish to annihilate them.

I admit, however, that I did not meet the Pathet Lao,
for after a struggle we prevailed in our refusal to accept
their credentials for the conference table. They may have
been entirely different in temper. These Pathet Lao were
communist guerrillas operating mainly in Phong Saly and
Sam Neua, the two northern provinces of the country.

Among those Laotians I did meet, patience and a
general reluctance to slit a neighbour's throat seeme dtobe
national traits. Certainly there is little of the crusader in
them, which may be why such a sad mess was made of

their policies by obstinate foreigners in the late fifties.

The Geneva Conference served Laos better than it could Vietnam. After much argument, Laos emerged with a neutral Government and, on balance, a weakened Pathet Lao. Chou En-Lai having accepted that France should have the right to keep her two military missions on Laotian soil, the Laotian Government were well content. No doubt they felt that the French would respect and support their neutral purpose. In this they were right, for the governments of France now adhered continuously to this policy through all vicissitudes. When, in 1961, President Kennedy discussed Laos with General de Gaulle in Paris, it can have been no surprise that the General strongly supported the idea of a neutral coalition under Souvanna Phouma.

The interval, however, had been troubled, not least because French opinions on South-East Asia had been much at a discount in Washington following the Geneva Conference. After prolonged and rather leisurely man-oeuvres, Prince Souvanna Phouma, as the head of the Royal Laotian Government, had contrived to come to terms with his half-brother Prince Souphannouvong at the head of the Pathet Lao. These were embodied in the Vientiane Agreements of November 1957, which provided for a neutral country under a coalition government.

The United States Government, which had hoped to see a more pro-western administration set up than that for which Prince Souvanna Phouma had openly declared, did not like this shift of events. Large sums of money had been spent, or were contemplated, to build up and equip the Royal Laotian army, some of this, it would seem, at the instant urging of the State Department and against the wiser counsel of the Department of Defence. American aid was denied to Souvanna Phouma, whose government fell in the summer of 1958. His successors, though further to the Right, were also more unfortunate. Despite American training and equipment, the Royal army was in no shape to take on the Pathet Lao at the Plaine des Jarres in the following May. The fighting was desultory rather than sharp, but it went badly for the government forces over the next two years.

A prudent attempt by Mr. Winthrop Brown, when newly appointed as American Ambassador, to bring neutralists and anti-communists together under Souvanna Phouma, accepting as a consequence a neutralist government again, was not supported in Washington, though both the French and British Governments favoured it. The delay and the mission of Mr. Graham Parsons to persuade Souvanna Phouma to abandon his policies were hardly propitious and achieved nothing. Not even a victory for a Washington sponsored leader of the Right, Phoumi Nosavan, based no doubt on sound American military advice, could redress the balance. By the end of 1960, Souvanna had fled to Cambodia, but was still recognized by Moscow and Peking, while the Pathet Lao were stronger than ever and reinforced by the defection of a local commander with his American equipment.

Two more years of negotiation followed, until the Geneva Neutralization Agreement [1] was signed in the summer of 1962. Meanwhile both Soviet and Chinese influence in Laos had increased significantly and a Soviet mission was installed in the capital.

More recent events have told against the communists.

[1] See below, p. 62.

Continuing efforts by the Vietcong to keep open their supply routes to their supporters in South Vietnam have resulted in hostilities and consequent suffering and loss to the local Laotian population. This has had its reaction in Vientiane where, for the present at least, the Vietcong and their allies the Pathet Lao are not loved. The final outcome in Laos will no doubt be deeply marked by the turn of events in Vietnam. Even so, the Laotians ask only to be let alone and, short of conquest, however Left their own government, they would not willingly accept Vietcong rule. They are entitled to this much surcease.

The moral of these chequered events would seem to be:

1.   That a country situated as is Laos geographically, with its two and a half million of population living in a territory half the size of France, with indifferent communications and no direct access to the sea, is well adapted to neutrality between two great power complexes. If, in these special conditions, neutrality suits Laos, it should suit the great powers also.

2.   If a people's temper is instinctively neutral, as was, and is, that of the Laotians, it is wise to try to match the policies of the western world to it. Nor can it be right to use economic aid to try to compel a community in such conditions to distort its policy. Where a nation offers no threat to the security of others, it should be safe from any form of coercion.

3.   Laos had over the years enjoyed better relations with the colonial power than any other part of Indo-China. In the light of this, and of the Chinese acceptance of two French bases on Laotian soil, it would have been prudent for the United States Government to have sought

and kept close relations with France in all Laotian affairs. Unfortunately the opposite was the practice. 'Nowhere else, perhaps', writes General Ely sadly, 'did France and Great Britain find themselves in such constant opposition to the United States about the policy to be pursued.'[2] General Ely's next comment is no less apposite: that the military and diplomatic representatives of the United States in Laos did not always see eye to eye.

There are occasions in diplomacy when to reach for the better is to lose the good.

The Cambodians

Cambodia, the smallest of the states in Indo-China, proved the toughest in negotiation at Geneva; it suspected all and yielded nothing. It is true that Vietminh penetration into that country had been the slightest and received scarcely more than token support from the Soviet or Chinese spokesmen. The speed and completeness of the renunciation and withdrawal were none the less a triumph for the Cambodian representatives.

The evening of 20-21 July is still vivid in my mind. The many phases of this intricate Geneva negotiation being almost all in order, Molotov and I, as co-chairmen of the Conference, came at last to the question of Cambodia. only to meet mistrust and stubborn negatives. Even the Three-Power Commission was viewed with scepticism, nor could General Bedell Smith's assurances, though generously given, prevail entirely.

[2] Paul Ely, *L'Indochine dans la tourmente* (Paris, Plon, 1964), p. 258.

It may have been exhaustion or a genuine fear that, if we did not finish during that night, all our work would be thrown back into confusion, but, whatever the cause, Molotov showed himself more responsive than I could have believed possible. Mr Sam Sary, the chief Cambodian delegate, had his way. He was given an agreeable programme on dates and time-table, and was reassured about his country's commitments under the Geneva accords.

This robust protagonist was soon to fall out with Norodom Sihanouk, his King, who was to step down from his throne to become Prime Minister. In this new role he pursued a course so devious as to perplex and sometimes to exasperate his foreign well-wishers. Through these twists and turns, more leftward than rightward, Sihanouk preserved two articles of faith intact. First, his country was to be truly neutral like Sweden or Switzerland, never to form part of a so-called neutralist block like Indonesia or Egypt; secondly, a neutrality guaranteed by the Geneva powers of 1954 held, in his conviction, the most hopeful promise for his people and his neighbours. It is still the best hope for peace, for all nations, that his faith should be fulfilled.

6

Twelve Points

THE following are the conclusions which can be drawn from my argument:

1. That the Geneva Agreements of 1954 can most usefully serve as the framework for the cease-fire negotiations and for the terms of any guaranteed settlement.

2. That the membership of the Geneva Conference should be retained, i.e. the United States, the U.S.S.R., China, the United Kingdom, France, Laos, Cambodia, North and South Vietnam.

3. That the co-chairmen of the Conference, the U.S.S.R. and the United Kingdom, should continue to function, their responsibilities being defined.

4. That the present membership of the Supervisory Commission, India, Canada and Poland, should be continued. The powers of the Commission should be defined and extended. It should be its responsibility to report its findings at stated intervals and in any emergency to the Conference, through the channel of the co-chairmen.

5. That any agreement should guarantee the territories and the neutrality of Laos and Cambodia, offering the same opportunity to South and North Vietnam.

6. That the guarantees should be endorsed by all the powers represented at the Conference.

7. That the guarantees to be offered to North and South Vietnam, Laos and Cambodia should be joint and several, on the Locarno model, the guarantors having the right in certain conditions to act without waiting for unanimity, should the terms of the agreement be violated.

8. That the guaranteed countries should be denied the purchase of arms from any guarantor power, this prohibition being supervised by the Commission.

9. That a sufficient period must be allowed to elapse after the cease-fire for the economy and security of South and North Vietnam to be established. A short-term neutralization scheme has no possibility of success. A period of ten to fifteen years should be allowed before South and North Vietnam are called upon to decide their mutual relationship. This term could be reduced by agreement between the two parties, the co-chairmen and the Commission.

10. That the scheme for the use of the waters of the Mekong river, now being prepared by the United Nations, should be prosecuted with the utmost despatch.

11. That the Geneva Prisoners of War Convention should be strictly observed.

12. That military plans and movements should be dovetailed into the political programme laid down by the Conference, whose first duty should be to give instructions for determining a cease-fire.

While the above proposals cannot bring an immediate solution to the political problems of Indo-China, nor one wholly satisfactory to any of the contending parties, they would make it possible for these territories, after twenty years of war, to cease to be a point of danger and to earn a better life in peace.

Select Documents

1. Indo-China: Attitude of Her Majesty's Government —paper prepared by the Foreign Secretary, Mr Anthony Eden, April 1954 [1]

1. We do not regard the London Communiqué [2] as committing us to join in immediate discussions on the possibility of Allied intervention in the Indo-China war.

2. We are not prepared to give any undertakings now, in advance of Geneva, concerning United Kingdom military action in Indo-China.

3. But we shall give all possible diplomatic support to the French Delegation at Geneva in efforts to reach an honourable settlement.

4. We can give an assurance now that if a settlement is reached at Geneva we shall join in guaranteeing that settlement and in setting up a collective defence in South-East Asia, as foreshadowed in the London Communiqué, to make that joint guarantee effective.

5. We hope that any Geneva settlement will make it possible for the joint guarantee to apply to at least the greater part of Indo-China.

6. If no such settlement is reached we shall be prepared at that time to consider with our Allies the action to be taken jointly in the situation then existing.

7. But we cannot give any assurance now about possible action on the part the United Kingdom in the event of

[1] Cmnd. 2834, p. 67.
[2] Communiqué issued by Mr Dulles and Mr Eden, 13 April 1954.

failure to reach agreement at Geneva for a cessation of hostilities in Indo-China.

8. We shall be ready to join with the United States Government now in studying measures to ensure the defence of Siam and the rest of South-East Asia, including Malaya, in the event of all or part of Indo-China being lost.

2. Extracts from Verbatim Record of Eighth Plenary Session of Geneva Conference on Indo-China, 21 July 1954 [1]

The Chairman (Mr Eden): As I think my colleagues are aware, agreement has now been reached on certain documents. It is proposed that this Conference should take note of these agreements. I accordingly propose to begin by reading out a list of the subjects covered by the documents, which I understand every delegation has in front of them.

First, agreement on the cessation of hostilities in Viet Nam; second, agreement on the cessation of hostilities in Laos; third, agreement on the cessation of hostilities in Cambodia. I would draw particular attention to the fact that these three agreements now incorporate the texts which were negotiated separately concerning the supervision of the Armistice in the three countries by the International Commission and the joint committees . . .

The further documents to which I must draw attention, which are in your possession, are: fourth, declaration by the Government of Laos on elections; fifth, declaration by the Government of Cambodia on elections and integration of all citizens into the national community; sixth, declaration by the Government of Laos on the military status of the country; seventh, declaration by the Government of Cambodia on the military status of the country; eighth, declaration by the Government of the French Republic on the withdrawal of troops from the three countries of Indochina.

Finally, gentlemen, there is the Draft Declaration by the Conference, which takes note of all these documents. I think

[1] Cmd. 9239, pp. 5-8.

all my colleagues have copies of this Draft Declaration before them. I will ask my colleagues in turn to express themselves upon this Declaration.

The Representative of France.

M. Mendès-France (France): Mr Chairman, the French Delegation approves the terms of this Declaration.

The Chairman: The Representative of Laos.

Mr Phoui Sananikone (Laos): The Delegation of Laos has no observations to make on this text.

The Chairman: The Representative of the People's Republic of China.

Mr Chou En-lai (People's Republic of China): We agree.

The Chairman: On behalf of Her Majesty's Government in the United Kingdom, I associate myself with the final Declaration of this Conference.

The Union of Soviet Socialist Republics.

M. Molotov (U.S.S.R.): The Soviet Delegation agrees.

The Chairman: The Representative of Cambodia.

Mr Tep Phan (Cambodia): The Delegation of Cambodia wishes to state that, among the documents just listed, one is missing. This is a Cambodian Declaration which we have already circulated to all delegations. . .

The Chairman: If this Declaration was not inscribed on the agenda on the list of documents I have read out, it is because it has only at this instant reached me. I do not think it is any part of the task of this Conference to deal with any past controversies in respect of the frontiers between Cambodia and Viet Nam.

The Representative of the Democratic Republic of Viet Nam.

Mr Pham van Dong (Democratic Republic of Viet Nam): Mr Chairman, I agree completely with the words pronounced by you. In the name of the Government of the Democratic Republic of Viet Nam we make the most express reservations regarding the statement made by the Delegation of Cambodia just now. I do this in the interests of good relations and under-standing between our two countries.

The Chairman: I think the Conference can take note of the statements of the Delegation of Cambodia just circulated and of the statement of the Representative of the Democratic Republic of Viet Nam.

I will continue calling upon countries to speak on the subject of the Declaration. I call upon the United States of America.

Mr Bedell Smith (United States): Mr Chairman, Fellow Delegates, as I stated to my colleagues during our meeting on July 18, my Government is not prepared to join in a Declaration by the Conference such as is submitted. However, the United States makes this unilateral declaration of its position in these matters:—

The Government of the United States being resolved to devote its efforts to the strengthening of peace in accordance with the principles and purposes of the United Nations

Takes Note

of the Agreements concluded at Geneva on July 20 and 21, 1954, between (*a*) the Franco-Laotian Command and the Command of the People's Army of Viet Nam; (*b*) the Royal Khmer Army Command and the Command of the People's Army of Viet Nam: (*c*) Franco-Vietnamese Command and the Command of the People's Army of Viet Nam, and of para-graphs 1 to 12 of the Declaration presented to the Geneva Conference on July 21, 1954.

The Government of the United States of America

Declares with regard to the aforesaid Agreements and paragraphs that (i) it will refrain from the threat or the use of force to disturb them, in accordance with Article 2 (Section 4) of the Charter of the United Nations dealing with the obliga-tion of Members to refrain in their international relations from the threat or use of force; and (ii) it would view any renewal of the aggression in violation of the aforesaid

Agreements with grave concern and as seriously threatening
international peace and security.

In connexion with the statement in the Declaration concerning free elections in Viet Nam, my Government wishes to
make clear its position which it has expressed in a Declaration
made in Washington on June 29, 1954, as follows:—

'In the case of nations now divided against their will,
we shall continue to seek to achieve unity through free
elections, supervised by the United Nations to ensure that
they are conducted fairly.'

With respect to the statement made by the Representative
of the State of Viet Nam, the United States reiterates its
traditional position that peoples are entitled to determine
their own future and that it will not join in an arrangement
which would hinder this. Nothing in its declaration just made
is intended to or does indicate any departure from this traditional position.

We share the hope that the agreement will permit Cambodia,
Laos and Viet Nam to play their part in full independence and
sovereignty, in the peaceful community of nations, and will
enable the peoples of that area to determine their own future.

Thank you, Mr Chairman.

The Chairman: The Conference will, I think, wish to take
note of the statement of the Representative of the United
States of America.

I call on the Representative of the State of Viet Nam.

Mr Tran van Do (State of Viet Nam): Mr Chairman, as
regards the final Declaration of the Conference, the Vietnamese Delegation requests the Conference to incorporate in
this Declaration after Article 10, the following text:—

'The Conference takes note of the Declaration of the
Government of the State of Viet Nam undertaking:

'to make and support every effort to re-establish a real
and lasting peace in Viet Nam:

'not to use force to resist the procedures for carrying the
cease-fire into effect, in spite of the objections and reservations

that the State of Viet Nam has expressed, especially in its final statement.'

The Chairman: I shall be glad to hear any views that my colleagues may wish to express. But, as I understand the position, the final Declaration has already been drafted and this additional paragraph has only just now been received; indeed, it has been amended since I received the text a few minutes ago. In all the circumstances, I suggest that the best course we can take is that the Conference should take note of the Declaration of the State of Viet Nam in this respect. If any of my colleagues has a contrary view, perhaps they would be good enough to say so. (None.) If none of my colleagues wishes to make any other observations, may I pass to certain other points which have to be settled before this Conference can conclude its labours?

The first is that, if it is agreeable to our colleagues, it is suggested that the two Chairmen should at the conclusion of this meeting address telegrams to the Governments of India, Poland and Canada to ask them if they will undertake the duties of supervision which the Conference has invited them to discharge. Is that agreeable? (Agreed.) Thank you.

The last is perhaps the least agreeable chapter of all our work. Certain costs arise from the decisions which the Conference has taken. It is suggested that it should be left here to your Chairmen as their parting gift to try to put before you some proposal in respect of those costs. I only wish to add in that connexion that, as this Conference is peculiar in not having any Secretariat in the usual sense of the term, the two Chairmen with considerable reluctance are prepared to undertake this highly invidious task. The costs to which I refer are not our own but those of the International Commission.

Does any delegate wish to make any further observation? (None.)

Gentlemen, perhaps I may say a final word as your Chairman for this day. We have now come to the end of our work. For a number of reasons it has been prolonged and intricate. The co-operation which all delegates have given to your two

Chairmen has enabled us to overcome many procedural difficulties. Without that co-operation, we could not have succeeded in our task. The Agreements concluded to-day could not, in the nature of things, give complete satisfaction to everyone. But they have made it possible to stop a war which has lasted for eight years and brought suffering and hardship to millions of people. They have also, we hope, reduced international tension at a point of instant danger to world peace. These results are surely worth our many weeks of toil. In order to bring about a cease-fire, we have drawn up a series of agreements. They are the best that our hands could devise. All will now depend upon the spirit in which those agreements are observed and carried out . . . .

3. Final Declaration of the Geneva Conference, 21 July 1954[1]

Final Declaration of the Geneva Conference on the problem of restoring peace in Indo-China, in which the representatives of Cambodia, the Democratic Republic of Vietnam, France, Laos, the People's Republic of China, the State of Vietnam, the Union of Soviet Socialist Republics, the United Kingdom and the United States of America took part.

1. The Conference takes note of the agreements ending hostilities in Cambodia, Laos and Viet-Nam and organising international control and the supervision of the execution of the provisions of these agreements.

2. The Conference expresses satisfaction at the ending of hostilities in Cambodia, Laos and Viet-Nam; the Conference expresses its conviction that the execution of the provisions set out in the present declaration and in the agreements on the cessation of hostilities will permit Cambodia, Laos and Viet-Nam henceforth to play their part, in full independence and sovereignty, in the peaceful community of nations.

3. The Conference takes note of the declarations made by the Governments of Cambodia and of Laos of their intention to adopt measures permitting all citizens to take their place in

[1] Cmd. 9239, pp. 83-85.

the national community, in particular by participating in the next general elections, which, in conformity with the constitution of each of these countries, shall take place in the course of the year 1955, by secret ballot and in conditions of respect for fundamental freedoms.

4. The Conference takes note of the clauses in the agreement on the cessation of hostilities in Viet-Nam prohibiting the introduction into Viet-Nam of foreign troops and military personnel as well as of all kinds of arms and munitions. The Conference also takes note of the declarations made by the Governments of Cambodia and Laos of their resolution not to request foreign aid, whether in war material, in personnel or in instructors except for the purpose of the effective defence of their territory and, in the case of Laos, to the extent defined by the agreements on the cessation of hostilities in Laos.

5. The Conference takes note of the clauses in the agreement on the cessation of hostilities in Viet-Nam to the effect that no military base under the control of a foreign State may be established in the regrouping zones of the two parties, the latter having the obligation to see that the zones allotted to them shall not constitute part of any military alliance and shall not be utilised for the resumption of hostilities or in the service of an aggressive policy. The Conference also takes note of the declarations of the Governments of Cambodia and Laos to the effect that they will not join in any agreement with other States if this agreement includes the obligation to participate in a military alliance not in conformity with the principles of the Charter of the United Nations or, in the case of Laos, with the principles of the agreement on the cessation of hostilities in Laos or, so long as their security is not threatened, the obligation to establish bases on Cambodian or Laotian territory for the military forces of foreign Powers.

6. The Conference recognises that the essential purpose of the agreement relating to Viet-Nam is to settle military questions with a view to ending hostilities and that the military demarcation line is provisional and should not in any way be interpreted as constituting a political or territorial boundary.

The Conference expresses its conviction that the execution of the provisions set out in the present declaration and in the agreement on the cessation of hostilities creates the necessary basis for the achievement in the near future of a political settlement in Viet-Nam.

7. The Conference declares that, so far as Viet-Nam is concerned, the settlement of political problems, effected on the basis of respect for the principles of independence, unity and territorial integrity, shall permit the Viet-Namese people to enjoy the fundamental freedoms, guaranteed by democratic institutions established as a result of free general elections by secret ballot. In order to ensure that sufficient progress in the restoration of peace has been made, and that all the necessary conditions obtain for free expression of the national will, general elections shall be held in July, 1956, under the supervision of an international commission composed of representatives of the member States of the International Supervisory Commission, referred to in the agreement on the cessation of hostilities. Consultations will be held on this subject between the competent representative authorities of the two zones from 20 July, 1955, onwards.

8. The provisions of the agreements on the cessation of hostilities intended to ensure the protection of individuals and of property must be most strictly applied and must, in particular, allow everyone in Viet-Nam to decide freely in which zone he wishes to live.

9. The competent representative authorities of the Northern and Southern zones of Viet-Nam, as well as the authorities of Laos and Cambodia, must not permit any individual or collective reprisals against persons who have collaborated in any way with one of the parties during the war, or against members of such persons' families.

10. The Conference takes note of the declaration of the Government of the French Republic to the effect that it is ready to withdraw its troops from the territory of Cambodia, Laos and Viet-Nam, at the request of the Governments concerned and within periods which shall be fixed by agreement

between the parties except in the cases where, by agreement between the two parties, a certain number of French troops shall remain at specified points and for a specified time.

11. The Conference takes note of the declaration of the French Government to the effect that for the settlement of all the problems connected with the re-establishment and consolidation of peace in Cambodia, Laos and Viet-Nam, the French Government will proceed from the principle of respect for the independence and sovereignty, unity and territorial integrity of Cambodia, Laos and Viet-Nam.

12. In their relations with Cambodia, Laos and Viet-Nam, each member of the Geneva Conference undertakes to respect the sovereignty, the independence, the unity and the territorial integrity of the above-mentioned States, and to refrain from any interference in their internal affairs.

13. The members of the Conference agree to consult one another on any question which may be referred to them by the International Supervisory Commission, in order to study such measures as may prove necessary to ensure that the agreements on the cessation of hostilities in Cambodia, Laos and Viet-Nam are respected.

4. Letter from President Eisenhower to the Prime Minister of the Republic of Vietnam, Mr Ngo Dinh Diem, regarding United States aid to Vietnam, 23 October 1954 [1]

I HAVE been following with great interest the course of developments in Viet-Nam, particularly since the conclusion of the conference at Geneva. The implications of the agreement concerning Viet-Nam have caused grave concern regarding the future of a country temporarily divided by an artificial military grouping, weakened by a long and exhausting war and faced with enemies without and by their subversive collaborators within.

Your recent requests for aid to assist in the formidable project of the movement of several hundred thousand loyal

[1] U.S. Dept. of State, *American Foreign Policy, 1950-5*; *Basic Documents*, (ii1957), pp. 2401-2.

Vietnamese citizens away from areas which are passing under a *de facto* rule and political ideology which they abhor, are being fulfilled. I am glad that the United States is able to assist in this humanitarian effort.

We have been exploring ways and means to permit our aid to Viet-Nam to be more effective and to make a greater contribution to the welfare and stability of the Government of Viet-Nam. I am, accordingly, instructing the American Ambassador to Viet-Nam to examine with you in your capacity as Chief of Government, how an intelligent program of American aid given directly to your Government can serve to assist Viet-Nam in its present hour of trial, provided that your Government is prepared to give assurances as to the standards of performance it would be able to maintain in the event such aid were supplied.

The purpose of this offer is to assist the Government of Viet-Nam in developing and maintaining a strong, viable state, capable of resisting attempted subversion or aggression through military means. The Government of the United States expects that this aid will be met by performance on the part of the Government of Viet-Nam in undertaking needed reforms. It hopes that such aid, combined with your own continuing efforts, will contribute effectively toward an independent Viet-Nam endowed with a strong government. Such a government would, I hope, be so responsive to the nationalist aspirations of its people, so enlightened in purpose and effective in performance, that it will be respected both at home and abroad and discourage any who might wish to impose a foreign ideology on your free people.

5. Messages despatched by the Co-Chairmen of the Geneva Conference to the two Governments in Vietnam, 8 May 1956 [1]

(*a*) *To the two Governments of Viet-Nam*

Acting with the authority of the Governments of the United

[1] Cmnd. 2834, pp. 96-97.

Kingdom and the Soviet Union, the Minister of State for
Foreign Affairs of Great Britain, Lord Reading, and the First
Deputy Foreign Minister of the U.S.S.R., M. A. A. Gromyko,
have met in London, as representatives of the two Co-
Chairmen of the Geneva Conference on Indo-China, and
have made a thorough examination of the problems relating
to the fulfilment of the Geneva Agreements in Viet-Nam. They
have also exchanged views on the proposal to convene a further
conference of members of the original Geneva Conference and
of the Supervisory Powers to discuss these problems.

2. In the course of these talks they expressed their concern
about the present situation in relation to the fulfilment of the
Geneva Agreements in Viet-Nam, where the implementation of
the political provisions of the Geneva Agreements has not yet
begun. In particular, consultations have not taken place about
the preparation and holding of free, nation-wide elections in
Viet-Nam under the supervision of an International Commission with a view to the re-establishment of the national unity
of Viet-Nam. There is thus at present a threat to the fulfilment
of this important provision of the Geneva Agreements, although both sides in Viet-Nam have accepted the principle of
national reunification by means of free general elections.

3. Pending the holding of free general elections for the
reunification of Viet-Nam, the two Co-Chairmen attach great
importance to the maintenance of the cease-fire under the
continued supervision of the International Commission for
Viet-Nam. They recognise that the dissolution of the French
Union High Command has increased the difficulties of the
International Supervisory Commission in Viet-Nam in carrying
out the functions specified in the Geneva Agreements, which
are the basis for the Commission's activities, and that these
difficulties must be overcome. The Co-Chairmen are confident
that the authorities in both parts of Viet-Nam will show effective
co-operation and that these difficulties will in practice be
removed.

4. Prompted by their desire to strengthen peace in Indo-
China on the basis of the principles and provisions of the

Geneva Agreements, the Co-Chairmen strongly urge the authorities of the Democratic Republic of Viet-Nam and those of the Republic of Viet-Nam to make every effort to implement the Geneva Agreements on Viet-Nam, to prevent any future violation of the military provisions of these agreements and also to ensure the implementation of the political provisions and principles embodied in the Final Declaration of the Geneva Conference. To this end the authorities of both parts of Viet-Nam are invited to transmit to the Co-Chairmen as soon as possible, either jointly or separately, their views about the time required for the opening of consultations on the organisation of nation-wide elections in Viet-Nam and the time required for the holding of elections as a means of achieving the unification of Viet-Nam.

5. Having noted with appreciation the valuable work performed by the International Supervisory Commission for Viet-Nam, the Co-Chairmen strongly urge the authorities in both parts of Viet-Nam to give the Commission all possible assistance in future in the exercise of their functions as defined by the Geneva Agreements on Viet-Nam.

6. The Co-Chairmen will continue to consult together about the situation in Viet-Nam and, if necessary in the light of that situation, they will also discuss the measures which should be taken to ensure the fulfilment of the Geneva Agreements on Viet-Nam, including the proposal to convene a new conference of the Members of the original Geneva Conference and of the States represented in the International Commissions in Indo-China.

6. Extracts from the Special Report to the Co-Chairmen of the Geneva Conference by the International Commission for Supervision and Control in Vietnam, Saigon, 2 June 1962 [1]

2. The International Commission has, from time to time, submitted to the Co-Chairmen Interim Reports giving a résumé of its activities as well as a brief review of the progress made by

[1] Cmnd. 1755, pp. 4-11.

the two Parties in the implementation of the provisions of the Agreement. . . .

3. In its 11th Interim Report, which covered the period from 1st February, 1960, to 28th February, 1961, the Commission had mentioned that, in spite of certain difficulties and the lurking dangers in Viet-Nam, the active presence of the Commission and its work had helped in preserving peace.

4. Since the presentation of the 11th Interim Report, the situation in Viet-Nam has shown signs of rapid deterioration. The Commission is obliged to make this Special Report to the Co-Chairmen with regard to the serious allegations of aggression and subversion on the part of the Democratic Republic of Viet-Nam against the Republic of Viet-Nam and the serious charges of violation of Articles 16, 17 and 19 of the Geneva Agreement by the Republic of Viet-Nam, in receiving military aid from the United States of America.

The Polish Delegation dissents from the views expressed in this Special Report. The Statement of the Polish Delegation is forwarded herewith. . . .

9. The Legal Committee has made a careful examination of the various allegations (against North Vietnam) and the evidence produced to support them, in the form of documents and other material evidence, and has made the following report, with the Polish Member dissenting: . . .

'(1) The Agreement on the Cessation of Hostilities in Viet-Nam proceeds on the principle of the complete cessation of all hostilities in Viet-Nam, respect by either Party of the Zone assigned to the other, and the inescapable responsibility of the Parties for the fulfilment of the obligations resulting therefrom.

Article 10 of the Agreement states expressly the obligation of the two Parties to order and *enforce* the *complete* cessation of all hostilities in Viet-Nam.

Article 19 of the Agreement casts the obligation on the two Parties to ensure that the Zones assigned to them are not used for the resumption of hostilities or to further an aggressive policy.

Article 24 of the Agreement proceeds on the principle of the inviolability of the Demilitarised Zone and the territories assigned to the two Parties and states expressly that the armed forces of each Party shall respect the territory under the military control of the other Party and shall commit no act and undertake no operation against the other Party.

Article 27 of the Agreement affirms expressly the responsibility of the Commanders of the Forces of the two Parties of ensuring full compliance with all the provisions of the Agreement by *all elements* and military personnel under their Command.

It follows that the using of one Zone for the organisation or the carrying out of any hostile activities in the other Zone, violations by members of the Armed Forces of one Party of the territory of the other Party, or the commission by any element under the control of one Party of any act directed against the other Party, would be contrary to the fundamental provisions of the Agreement which enjoin mutual respect for the territories assigned to the two Parties.

(2) Having examined the complaints and the supporting material sent by the South Vietnamese Mission, the Committee has come to the conclusion that in specific instances there is evidence to show that armed and unarmed personnel, arms, munitions and other supplies have been sent from the Zone in the North to the Zone in the South with the object of supporting, organizing and carrying out hostile activities, including armed attacks, directed against the Armed Forces and Administration of the Zone in the South. These acts are in violation of Articles 10, 19, 24 and 27 of the Agreement on the Cessation of Hostilities in Viet-Nam.

(3) In examining the complaints and the supporting material, in particular documentary material sent by the South Vietnamese Mission, the Committee has come to the further conclusion that there is evidence to show that the

[People's Army of Vietnam] has allowed the Zone in the North to be used for inciting, encouraging and supporting hostile activities in the Zone in the South, aimed at the overthrow of the Administration in the South. The use of the Zone in the North for such activities is in violation of Articles 19, 24 and 27 of the Agreement on the Cessation of Hostilities in Viet-Nam.

(4) The Committee considers that further investigation is necessary to reach a final conclusion as to whether the kidnapping and murder of Colonel Nam, late Chief of the South Vietnamese Mission, was a part of the activities referred to in sub-paragraphs (2) and (3) above and prohibited under Articles 19, 24 and 27 of the Agreement. The South Vietnamese Mission has furnished *prima facie* evidence to warrant such a full investigation of the case by the Commission.

We shall submit in due course a full report setting out in detail the complaints made by the South Vietnamese Mission, the evidence forwarded in relation to these complaints, and our specific observations thereon.'

10. The Commission accepts the conclusions reached by the Legal Committee that there is sufficient evidence to show beyond reasonable doubt that the [People's Army of Vietnam] has violated Articles 10, 19, 24 and 27 in specific instances. The Polish Delegation dissents from these conclusions. On the basis of the fuller report, that is being prepared by the Legal Committee covering all the allegations and incidents, the Commission will take action as appropriate in each individual case.

11. Concurrently with the developments referred to in paragraphs 7 and 8 above, and subsequently, the Commission received communications from the [People's Army of Vietnam] High Command and its Liaison Mission alleging direct military intervention in South Viet-Nam by the Government of the United States of America, and ever-increasing import of war material and introduction of military personnel in violation of

the Geneva Agreement. The allegations, amongst others, were:

(a) the conclusion of a bilateral military Agreement between President Ngo Dinh Diem and United States Ambassador Nolting;

(b) the gradual introduction of about 5,000 United States military personnel into South Viet-Nam, 'which will soon be increased to 8,000';

(c) the arrival of four aircraft carriers—*Core, Breton, Princeton* and *Croaton*—on different occasions, bringing in helicopters, other aircraft, military equipment and military personnel;

(d) the introduction by the United States of America of approximately four companies of helicopters, many jet fighters, fighters/fighter bombers and transport planes, along with military vehicles and other stores;

(e) the visits of a large number of high United States military experts and dignitaries to Saigon for inspection and guidance, particularly those of General Maxwell Taylor, Admiral H. Felt and General Lemnitzer;

(f) the establishment of a United States Military Assistance Command, with a four-star General, Paul D. Harkins, as its Chief.

12. Since December 1961 the Commission's Teams in South Viet-Nam have been persistently denied the right to control and inspect, which are part of the mandatory tasks. Thus, these Teams, though they were able to observe the steady and continuous arrival of war material, including aircraft carriers with helicopters on board, were unable, in view of the denial of controls, to determine precisely the quantum and nature of war material unloaded and introduced into South Viet-Nam....

17. As the Commission has been denied mandatory controls, ... it has not been able to make a precise assessment of the number of military personnel and the quantum of war material brought in. However, from 3rd December, 1961, up to 5th May, 1962, the Commission's Teams have controlled

the entry of 72 military personnel, and observed but not controlled 173 military personnel, 62 helicopters, 6 reconnaissance aircraft, 5 jet aircraft, 57 fighters/fighter bombers, 25 transport aircraft, 26 unspecified types of aircraft, 102 jeeps, 8 tractors, 8 105-mm. howitzers, 3 armoured carriers (tracked), 29 armoured fighting vehicle trailers, 404 other trailers, and radar equipment and crates, 5 warships, 9 LSTs (including 4 visiting LSTs), 3 LCTs, 5 visiting aircraft carriers and spares of various kinds. In respect of some of the instances of import of war materials between 3rd December, 1961 and 16th January, 1962, violations under Article 17 (*e*) as well as violation of Article 25, have been recorded against the Republic of Viet-Nam for its failure to notify arrivals and imports as required by the Geneva Agreement, and for not affording all possible assistance to the Commission's Teams in the performance of their tasks.

18. In regard to claims for credits made by the Southern Party in justification of certain imports, the Commission wishes to point out that in so far as major items of war material are concerned, except in a limited number of cases, there is no established credit in favour of the Republic of Viet-Nam. On the other hand, for some of these items, there is already a debit against it. In this context, it must be borne in mind that, even where credit exists, according to Article 17(*b*) of the Agreement, the Party can only import war material 'piece-for-piece of the same type and with similar characteristics'. However, controls not having been permitted, the Commission is not in a position to satisfy itself whether this essential requirement has in fact been fulfilled even in cases where credit exists.

19. As regards the allegation of the [People's Army of Vietnam] High Command that a U.S. Military Assistance Command has been set up in South Viet-Nam in violation of Article 19, the Commission requested the Party to furnish the following information:

    (i) whether such a U.S. Command has been set up;

    (ii) the basis on which it has been established;

    (iii) the purpose for which it has been constituted;

(iv) its strength;
(v) the scope of its activities.

The South Vietnamese Mission in its letter dated 15th March, 1962, has not furnished the necessary information required by the Commission, other than stating that this Military Assistance Command is not a military command in the usual sense of the term, and that its only function is to supervise and manage the utilisation of American personnel and equipment. The Mission stated further that there was no military alliance between the United States of America and the Republic of Viet-Nam as no treaty of this nature had been ratified by either Government.

20. Taking all the facts into consideration, and basing itself on its own observations and authorised statements made in the United States of America and the Republic of Viet-Nam, the Commission concludes that the Republic of Viet-Nam has violated Articles 16 and 17 of the Geneva Agreement in receiving the increased military aid from the United States of America in the absence of any established credit in its favour. The Commission is also of the view that, though there may not be any formal military alliance between the Governments of the United States of America and the Republic of Viet-Nam, the establishment of a U.S. Military Assistance Command in South Viet-Nam, as well as the introduction of a large number of U.S. military personnel beyond the stated strength of the MAAG (Military Assistance Advisory Group), amounts to a factual military alliance, which is prohibited under Article 19 of the Geneva Agreement. . . .

22. The International Commission wishes to draw the serious and earnest attention of the Co-Chairmen to the gravity of the situation that has developed in Viet-Nam in the last few months. Fundamental provisions of the Geneva Agreement have been violated by both Parties, resulting in ever-increasing tension and threat of resumption of open hostilities. In this situation, the role of the Commission for the maintenance of peace in Viet-Nam is being greatly hampered because of denial of co-operation by both the Parties. . . .

7. Declaration on the Neutrality of Laos, Geneva, 23 July 1962 [1]

The Governments of the Union of Burma, the Kingdom of Cambodia, Canada, the People's Republic of China, the Democratic Republic of Viet-Nam, the Republic of France, the Republic of India, the Polish People's Republic, the Republic of Viet-Nam, the Kingdom of Thailand, the Union of Soviet Socialist Republics, the United Kingdom of Great Britain and Northern Ireland and the United States of America, whose representatives took part in the International Conference on the Settlement of the Laotian Question, 1961-1962;

Welcoming the presentation of the statement of neutrality by the Royal Government of Laos of July 9, 1962, and taking note of this statement, which is, with the concurrence of the Royal Government of Laos, incorporated in the present Declaration as an integral part thereof, and the text of which is as follows:

The Royal Government of Laos,

Being resolved to follow the path of peace and neutrality in conformity with the interests and aspirations of the Laotian people, as well as the principles of the Joint Communiqué of Zurich dated June 22, 1961, and of the Geneva Agreements of 1954, in order to build a peaceful, neutral, independent, democratic, unified and prosperous Laos.

Solemnly declares that:

(1) It will resolutely apply the five principles of peaceful co-existence in foreign relations, and will develop friendly relations and establish diplomatic relations with all countries, the neighbouring countries first and foremost, on the basis of equality and of respect for the independence and sovereignty of Laos;

(2) It is the will of the Laotian people to protect and ensure respect for the sovereignty, independence, neutrality, unity, and territorial integrity of Laos;

(3) It will not resort to the use or threat of force in any way

[1] Cmnd. 2834, pp. 178-81.

which might impair the peace of other countries, and will not interfere in the internal affairs of other countries;

(4) It will not enter into any military alliance or into any agreement, whether military or otherwise, which is inconsistent with the neutrality of the Kingdom of Laos; it will not allow the establishment of any foreign military bases on Laotian territory, nor allow any country to use Laotian territory for military purposes or for the purposes of interference in the internal affairs of other countries, nor recognise the protection of any alliance or military coalition, including SEATO;

(5) It will not allow any foreign interference in the internal affairs of the Kingdom of Laos in any form whatsoever;

(6) Subject to the provisions of Article 5 of the Protocol, it will require the withdrawal from Laos of all foreign troops and military personnel, and will not allow any foreign troops or military personnel to be introduced into Laos;

(7) It will accept direct and unconditional aid from all countries that wish to help the Kingdom of Laos build up an independent and autonomous national economy on the basis of respect for the sovereignty of Laos;

(8) It will respect the treaties and agreements signed in conformity with the interests of the Laotian people and of the policy of peace and neutrality of the Kingdom, in particular the Geneva Agreements of 1962, and will abrogate all treaties and agreements which are contrary to those principles.

This statement of neutrality by the Royal Government of Laos shall be promulgated constitutionally and shall have the force of law.

The Kingdom of Laos appeals to all the States participating in the International Conference on the Settlement of the Laotian Question, and to all other States, to recognise the sovereignty, independence, neutrality, unity, and territorial integrity of Laos, to conform to these principles in all respects, and to refrain from any action inconsistent therewith.

Confirming the principles of respect for the sovereignty, independence, unity and territorial integrity of the Kingdom of Laos and non-interference in its internal affairs which are embodied in the Geneva Agreements of 1954:

Emphasising the principle of respect for the neutrality of the Kingdom of Laos;

Agreeing that the above-mentioned principles constitute a basis for the peaceful settlement of the Laotian question;

Profoundly convinced that the independence and neutrality of the Kingdom of Laos will assist the peaceful democratic development of the Kingdom of Laos and the achievement of national accord and unity in that country, as well as the strengthening of peace and security in South-East Asia;

1. Solemnly declare, in accordance with the will of the Government and people of the Kingdom of Laos, as expressed in the statement of neutrality by the Royal Government of Laos of 9 July, 1962, that they recognise and will respect and observe in every way the sovereignty, independence, neutrality, unity and territorial integrity of the Kingdom of Laos.

2. Undertake, in particular, that

(a) they will not commit or participate in any way in any act which might directly or indirectly impair the sovereignty, independence, neutrality, unity or territorial integrity of the Kirgdom of Laos;

(b) they will not resort to the use or threat of force or any other measure which might impair the peace of the Kingdom of Laos;

(c) they will refrain from all direct or indirect interference in the internal affairs of the Kingdom of Laos;

(d) they will not attach conditions of a political nature to any assistance which they may offer or which the Kingdom of Laos may seek;

(e) they will not bring the Kingdom of Laos in any way into any military alliance or any other agreement, whether military or otherwise, which is inconsistent with her neutrality, nor invite or encourage her to enter into any such alliance or to conclude any such agreement;

(*f*) they will respect the wish of the Kingdom of Laos not to recognise the protection of any alliance or military coalition, including SEATO;

(*g*) they will not introduce into the Kingdom of Laos foreign troops or military personnel in any form whatsoever, nor will they in any way facilitate or connive at the introduction of any foreign troops or military personnel;

(*h*) they will not establish nor will they in any way facilitate or connive at the establishment in the Kingdom of Laos of any foreign military base, foreign strong point or other foreign installation of any kind;

(*i*) they will not use the territory of the Kingdom of Laos for interference in the internal affairs of other countries;

(*j*) they will not use the territory of any country, including their own, for interference in the internal affairs of the Kingdom of Laos.

3. Appeal to all other States to recognise, respect and observe in every way the sovereignty, independence and neutrality, and also the unity and territorial integrity, of the Kingdom of Laos and to refrain from any action inconsistent with these principles or with other provisions of the present Declaration.

4. Undertake, in the event of a violation or threat of violation of the sovereignty, independence, neutrality, unity or territorial integrity of the Kingdom of Laos, to consult jointly with the Royal Government of Laos and among themselves in order to consider measures which might prove to be necessary to ensure the observance of these principles and the other provisions of the present Declaration.

5. The present Declaration shall enter into force on signature and together with the statement of neutrality by the Royal Government of Laos of July 9, 1962 shall be regarded as constituting an international agreement. The present Declaration shall be deposited in the archives of the Governments of the United Kingdom and the Union of Soviet Socialist Republics, which shall furnish certified copies thereof

to the other signatory States and to all the other States of the world.

In witness whereof, the undersigned Plenipotentiaries have signed the present Declaration.

Done in two copies in Geneva this twenty-third day of July one thousand nine hundred and sixty-two in the English, Chinese, French, Laotian and Russian languages, each text being equally authoritative.

8. North Vietnam's Attitude to Negotiations[1]

Excerpts from article by Nguyen Van Vinh, member of the Central Committee of the Vietnam Workers' Party and Chairman of the Democratic Republic of Vietnam State Committee for National Reunification, in Vietnam Courier *(Hanoi), 27 Sept. 1965*

. . . Comrade Pham Van Dong, VDR [Democratic Republic of Vietnam] Premier, has put forth a fourpoint programme on the settlement of the South Vietnam problem: 1. Recognition of the basic national rights of the Vietnamese people: peace, independence, sovereignty, unity and territorial integrity. According to the Geneva agreements, the U.S. Government must withdraw from South Vietnam all U.S. troops, military personnel and weapons of all kinds, dismantle all U.S. bases there, cancel its military alliance with South Vietnam. It must end its policy of intervention and aggression in South Vietnam. According to the Geneva agreements, the U.S. Government must stop its acts of war against North Vietnam, completely cease all encroachments upon the territory and sovereignty of the VDR.

2. Pending the peaceful reunification, while Vietnam is still temporarily divided into two zones, the military provisions of the 1954 Geneva agreements on Vietnam must be strictly respected: the two zones must refrain from joining any military alliance with foreign countries, there must be no foreign military bases, troops and military personnel in their respective territory.

[1] BBC, *Summary of World Broadcasts*, FE 1971 A3-4, 28 Sept. 1965.

3. The internal affairs of South Vietnam must be settled by the South Vietnamese people themselves, in accordance with the programme of the SVNLF, without any foreign interference.

4. The peaceful reunification of Vietnam is to be settled by the Vietnamese people in both zones, without any foreign interference.

The Government of the VDR is of the view that the above-expounded stand is the basis for the soundest political settlement of the Vietnam problem. If this basis is recognised, favourable conditions will be created for the peaceful settlement of the Vietnam problem and it will be possible to consider the reconvening of an international conference along the pattern of the 1954 Geneva Conference on Vietnam.

With regard to the above-mentioned points raised by South and North Vietnam, certain people ask: Now that the U.S.A. has proposed unconditional discussions, why does Vietnam put forward terms and compel U.S.A. to accept them? No, the Geneva agreements are not the conditions advanced by us unilaterally but a treaty accepted by all parties concerned. These are conditions which both sides have pledged themselves to respect and implement. That is why we take the Geneva agreements as a basis and resolutely oppose their distortion and sabotage by the U.S.A.

Concerning the immediate goals of the struggle, which are [the] national rights of the South Vietnamese people—namely independence, democracy, peace and neutrality with a view to reunifying the country, as expounded in the programme of the SVNLF [South Vietnam National Liberation Front]—the U.S. imperialists must absolutely recognise them because this is already a much [lesser] price which the SVNLF and the Vietnam Fatherland Front compel the U.S. imperialists to pay in comparison with a number of provisions of the Geneva agreements on Vietnam. In fact, should these agreements be strictly implemented, Vietnam would have been reunified as early as 1956. . . . Together with their northern compatriots, the southern people would have built for years a peaceful, unified, independent, democratic and prosperous Vietnam. At

present, the SVNLF only demands a neutral South Vietnam.
As far as the reunification of Vietnam is concerned, the
People's Fronts in both zones undertake to realise it step by
step in accordance with the aspirations of the entire people.
Is it not clear that, compared with the Geneva agreements,
this is a much lower price, which the U.S. imperialists must pay
to settle their debts? Is it not clear that it is a[n] honourable
way out for them? . . .

Generally speaking, when provoking an aggressive war
against a country, the imperialists must introduce their troops
into that country first, and when they want to stop their war
and seek peace they must withdraw their troops. This is quite
easily understandable. Thus, to attain a political solution and
genuine peace in South Vietnam, the U.S. imperialists must
first of all accept to withdraw their troops. As for how this
withdrawal will be carried out, the imperialist camp has had a
lot of experiences such as the withdrawal of the French troops
from Indochina and Algeria, of the Americans from Laos and
other parts of the world.

. . . It is sheer illusion if it [the U.S.A.] expects to exchange
the withdrawal of U.S. and satellite troops from South Vietnam
for that of the South Vietnam liberation army, whom they
slanderously called North Vietnamese troops. The workers,
peasants and other labouring people in South Vietnam now
taking up arms to fight U.S. imperialist aggression will go
nowhere. They will continue to fight in their fields and in their
native villages. There will be no question of a new regroup-
ment to the North as did in 1954 the Vietnam People's Army
units operating south of the 17th parallel. Only the U.S.
imperialists and their satellites, the only foreign troops, should
get out of South Vietnam. If the U.S. imperialists continue
their aggression against South Vietnam and refuse to withdraw,
all the South Vietnamese who, over 10 years ago, went to North
Vietnam with arms under the terms of the Geneva agreements
and in implementation of the armistice clause, will return to
South Vietnam to fight beside their kith-and-kin when called
upon to do so by the SVNLF. . . .

If we do not solve the South Vietnam problem on the basis of these fundamental conditions put forth by the people of the two zones of Vietnam and if we accept the U.S. imperialists' unconditional discussions offer, this would be tantamount to coming to the conference table to recognize their aggression and their permanent presence in South Vietnam and negotiate under the pressure of their bombs.

9. The United States Attitude to Negotiations [1]

I. The Fact of Aggression

The simple fact is that tens of thousands of trained and armed men, including units of the North Vietnamese regular army, have been sent by Hanoi into South Vietnam for the purpose of imposing Hanoi's will on South Vietnam by force. It is this external aggression which is responsible for the presence of U.S. combat forces. Indeed, it was not until the early summer of 1965 that the number of U.S. military personnel in South Vietnam reached the number of those which have been infiltrated by Hanoi. If this aggression from the outside were removed, U.S. combat forces would not be needed.

II. The U.S. Commitment

The United States has a clear and direct commitment to the security of South Vietnam against external attack. This commitment is based upon bilateral agreements between the United States and South Vietnam, upon the SEATO treaty (whose obligations are both joint and several), upon annual actions by the Congress in providing aid to South Vietnam, upon the policy expressed in such Congressional action as the August 1964 resolution, and upon the solemn declarations of three U.S. Presidents. At stake is not just South Vietnam, nor even South-East Asia; there is also at stake the integrity of a U.S. commitment and the importance of that commitment to the peace right around the globe.

III. Initiatives for Peace

A. We are not aware of any initiative which has been taken

[1] White House paper, 'The Heart of the Matter in Vietnam,' 4 Jan. 1966 (U.S. Information Service, London).

by Hanoi during the past five years to seek peace in South-East Asia. Reports of 'peace feelers' have to do with initiatives by third parties. Hanoi has denied that it has ever made any 'peace feelers'. We ourselves know of none. During 1965 Hanoi has consistently insisted that its four points must be accepted as the sole basis for peace in Vietnam. The third of these four points would require the imposition of the programme of the Liberation Front upon South Vietnam, whether the South Vietnamese wanted it or not.

B. The initiatives for peace undertaken by our side, and by many other governments, would be hard to count. They began with President Kennedy's talk with Premier Khrushchev in Vienna in June 1961 and have not ceased. The publicly-known initiatives have been multiplied many times by private initiatives not yet disclosed. On the public record, however, are the following instances:

1. Kennedy-Khrushchev talks in June 1961;

2. Geneva Conference on Laos;

3. U.S. reference of Gulf of Tonkin matter to the U.N. Security Council in August 1964;

4. The Polish proposal to convene the two co-chairmen and the three members of the ICC (India, Canada and Poland) to take up the question of Laos;

5. The call of 17 non-aligned nations for negotiations without preconditions;

6. Attempts by U Thant to visit Hanoi and Peking;

7. President Johnson's call for unconditional discussions;

8. The British Commonwealth Committee on Vietnam;

9. Attempted or actual visits by Patrick Gordon Walker, Mr Davis (MP), and Ghanaian delegation.

IV. U.S. Contributions to the Basket of Peace

The following statements are on the public record about elements which the U.S. believes can go into peace in South-East Asia:

1. The Geneva Agreements of 1954 and 1962 are an adequate basis for peace in South-East Asia;

2. We would welcome a conference on South-East Asia or on any part thereof;

3. We would welcome 'negotiations without pre-conditions' as the 17 nations put it;

4. We would welcome unconditional discussions as President Johnson put it;

5. A cessation of hostilities could be the first order of business at a conference or could be the subject of preliminary discussions;

6. Hanoi's four points could be discussed along with other points which others might wish to propose;

7. We want no U.S. bases in South-East Asia;

8. We do not desire to retain U.S. troops in South Vietnam after peace is assured;

9. We support free elections in South Vietnam to give the South Vietnamese a Government of their own choice;

10. The question of reunification of Vietnam should be determined by the Vietnamese through their own free decisions;

11. The countries of South-East Asia can be non-aligned or neutral if that be their option;

12. We would much prefer to use our resources for the economic reconstruction of South-East Asia than in war. If there is peace, North Vietnam could participate in a regional effort to which we would be prepared to contribute at least one billion dollars;

13. The President has said 'the Viet Cong would have no difficulty in being represented and having their views presented if Hanoi for a moment decides she wants to cease aggression. And I would not think that would be an insurmountable problem at all.'

14. We have said publicly and privately that we could stop the bombing of North Vietnam as a step toward peace although there has not been the slightest hint or suggestion from the other side as to what they would do if the bombing stopped.

In other words we have put everything into the basket of peace except the surrender of South Vietnam.